The Bloody
BARON

WHO WAS...

The Bloody BARON

Evil Invader of the East

NICK MIDDLETON

✱ SHORT BOOKS

This edition published in 2004 by
Short Books
15 Highbury Terrace
London N5 1UP

10 9 8 7 6 5 4 3 2

Copyright ©
Nick Middleton 2001

Nick Middleton has asserted his right under the Copyright,
Designs and Patents Act 1988 to be identified as the
author of this work. All rights reserved. No part of this
publication may be reproduced, stored in a retrieval
system or transmitted in any form, or by any means
(electronic, mechanical, or otherwise) without
the prior written permission of both the copyright
owners and the publisher.

First published in Great Britain
by Short Books Ltd in 2001

A CIP catalogue record for this book
is available from the British Library.

ISBN 1-904095-87-9

Printed in Great Britain by
Bookmarque, Croydon, Surrey.

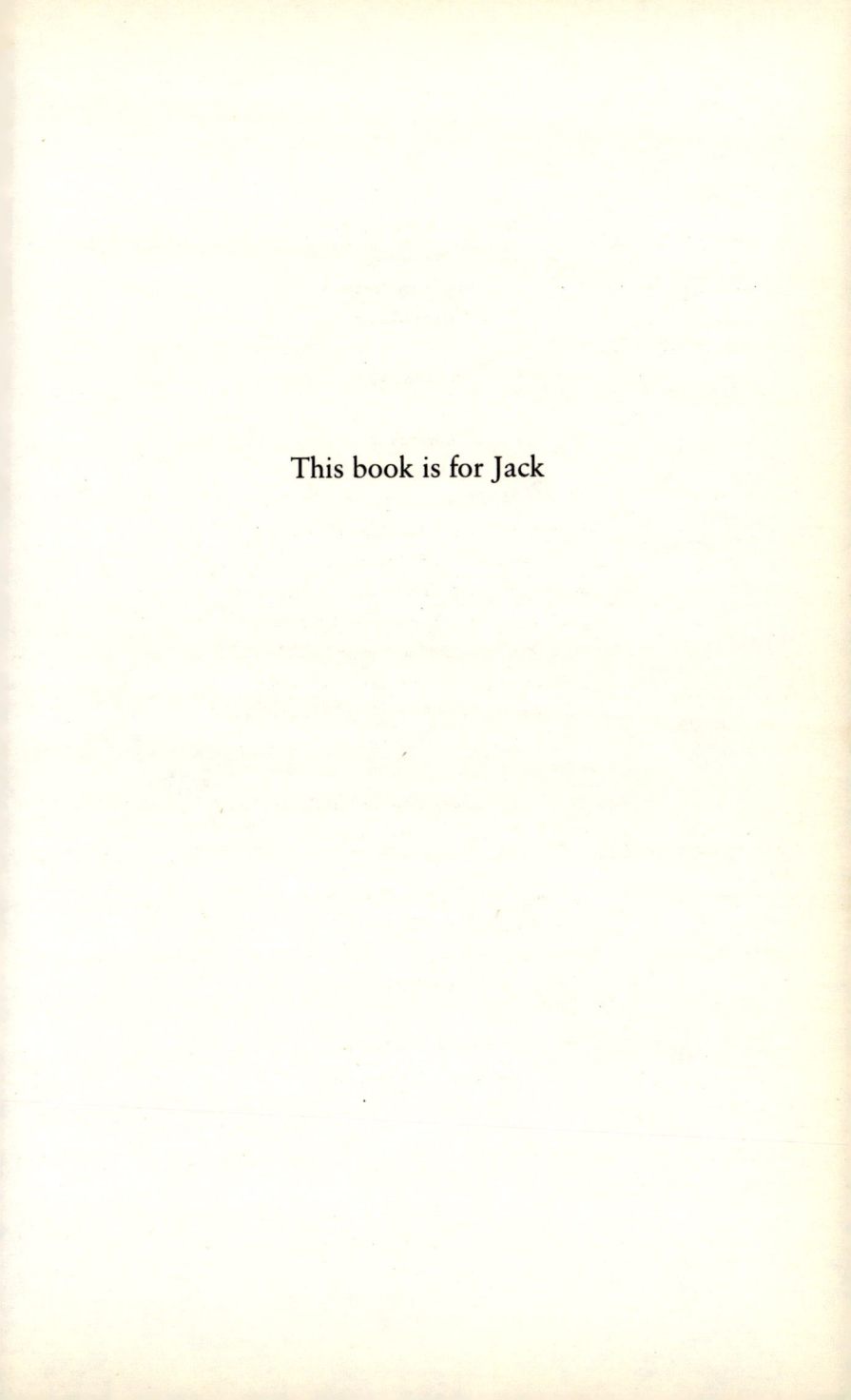

This book is for Jack

Chapter One

The mysterious visitor

Mongolia, 1921: night was falling as Baron von Ungern-Sternberg paced up and down inside his tent rapping his long whip against his riding boots and muttering dark words to himself. He thought about sending out for some men to flog, but he decided their screams would only aggravate his headache. So he paced up and down and muttered some more.'

Just at that moment, there was a shout from outside the Baron's tent. It was the Baron's personal military assistant, or adjutant, a man by the name of Teapot who had a square head the shape of a loaf of bread.

'Your Excellency!' cried Teapot.

'What is it?' snapped the Baron.

'Your Excellency. A horseman,' replied Teapot's voice.

'About time too,' the Baron muttered to himself as he heard the sound of a galloping horse, its hooves thudding on the cold, hard ground outside. 'Send him straight in,' he shouted to Teapot, 'and then leave us alone.'

After a little while, the door of the Baron's tent swung open, letting in a blast of cold air that made the flames of the fire flicker, sending shadows dancing on the pale, material walls. A tinkle of bells heralded the arrival of a man who ducked inside and stood facing the Baron, but not looking at him. The man's eyes glanced briefly around the insides of the tent; he then folded his leg underneath him to sit down on his heel.

The Baron stooped and sat down to study

the strange figure before him. He wore a long black leather coat and a bushy cap of animal hide decorated with coloured feathers that hung down in front of his face. Around his middle was tied a bright orange silk sash and from this sash hung bunches of leather straps. Some of the straps had small bells on the end, others had pieces of metal on them. In his left hand he held a long wooden stick, the top of which was carved into the shape of a horse's head.

The Baron's tent was a large one, and was made of thick white felt, wrapped around a wooden lattice that looked like an extra large climbing frame. It was pitched in the middle of a vast grassy plain in Mongolia, a country deep in the heart of Central Asia, where the winter nights are very cold. Most Mongolians live in tents like this one. While outside, the bitter winds sweep across the steppe, inside the tents are always warm and snug thanks to the fire that burns in the middle. Above the fire stands a chimney that takes the smoke up and out through a hole in the ceiling.

The Baron was a Russian by birth, but he had been in Mongolia for some weeks now, leading his motley army of Russian deserters and local recruits towards the city of Urga, Mongolia's capital. He was rather puny to look at, with an abnormally small head and very long hands. His face was very white, he had a huge bushy moustache, and one eye a little above the other. But although he looked weak, the Baron had an iron constitution and ruthless energy. He had fought in several duels, one of which had left him with a terrible sabre scar on his forehead which pulsed with red veins when he got angry. It had been pulsing while he waited for the man in the long, black leather coat to arrive.

For most of the afternoon the Baron had been studying maps and charts, trying to decide the best route to Urga. His small army had been riding their horses towards Urga for days, but the Baron thought that they should have arrived by now. The problem was that the maps weren't very good ones. This annoyed the Baron, and it was his annoyance that had brought on the headache.

'Useless maps!' he had screamed in his strangely high-pitched voice as he lashed at them with his whip, sending pieces of paper shooting off in every direction.

All the Baron's men were frightened of him, and with good reason. He came from a long line of fighting men. Among his ancestors were Baron Heinrich, a wandering knight whose nickname was the 'Axe', and the 18th-century Baron Wilhelm who was called the 'Brother of Satan'. Another was known as 'Peter the Wrecker'.

The Baron himself had also had lots of practice at killing people during his military career and was very good at it. When he entered a café, the other customers usually made a hasty exit, since he was an expert with his gun and had shot many fellow officers during his heavy drinking bouts. He was also a specialist in flogging. His violent nature had led his men to call him the 'Bloody Baron', but they never dared to use this nickname while the Baron himself was in earshot.

The Bloody Baron wasn't used to being polite to people, since most of the visitors to his tent were soldiers who came to be punished, so he didn't say hello to the man crouched in front of him. He did, however, offer him some tea, and filled a bowl from the big iron kettle that stood on the fire.

The man stretched out to take the bowl, making his bells tinkle, and proceeded to slurp his tea very loudly, which was the custom in Mongolia. Still, neither man had spoken, and the only other sound that could be heard inside the tent was the crackling of the fire.

When he had finished the tea, the man in the black leather coat put the bowl on the ground and carefully placed his horsehead stick beside it. He dug into the orange sash around his middle and very slowly pulled out a small leather pouch. He opened it and carefully tipped on to the ground in front of him a pile of small bird bones and some dried grass. He looked up and fixed the Baron with his eyes, staring for what seemed like a very long time.

Without taking his eyes off the Baron for even a moment, the man grabbed a tuft of the dried grass and threw it into the fire. This he followed with another tuft, and another, until the whole tent was filled with a sweet smell that made the Baron remember the time when, as a child, he had tried to set fire to a haystack near his home in Estonia.

The man in the black leather coat was still staring at the Baron when he picked up the bird bones and tossed them into the flames. He stared and he stared, his eyes appearing to get bigger and bigger, as the bones crackled in the fire.

After about ten minutes, the man reached his hand into the flames and pulled out the bones. They were all burnt and fractured, and the man in the black coat took his eyes off the Baron to gaze intently at the bones.

For the first time since he had set foot in the Baron's tent, the man began to speak.

'You will ride south, and cross a great range of mountains before coming to the Sacred Monastery.'

The Baron knew that this was what Mongolians called the city of Urga. He had asked many herders for directions over the last few days, and none of them had understood when he said he wanted to go to Urga, but when he said the Sacred Monastery, they all knew what he was talking about.

'You will pull back, to a river half a day's ride from the Sacred Monastery, and there you will camp for seven days and seven nights,' the man in the black leather coat continued. 'Then will be the time to strike. The hills will be set alight with a thousand fires and the Sacred Monastery surrounded by a sea of blood.'

He coughed and suddenly his hand came out and swept the charred bird bones away. Without looking again at the Baron, the man in the black leather coat picked up his horsehead stick, rose to his feet, and pushed open the door to disappear into the night with a tinkle of bells.

As Baron von Ungern-Sternberg lay down on his blanket to sleep (he never carried a bed on military campaigns), he heard the far-off sound of a wolf howling at the moon. The Bloody Baron liked the idea of a sea of blood, but he wondered what the man in the black leather coat had meant by the thousand fires. The last thing to pass through his mind before he drifted off to sleep was that his headache had gone.

Chapter Two

The Baron's Grand Plan

The following morning the Bloody Baron was up bright and early to give the order for his men to break camp and saddle their horses. He wanted to be on his way as quickly as possible, so there was no time for breakfast. Groups of his men ran off in all directions when they heard the order. One team had the job of rounding up all the sheep that the Baron's army kept with them to provide food. Another group began loading the carts with cooking stoves, guns and ammunition, while Teapot supervised the Baron's personal bodyguards in dismantling the Baron's tent and putting it on to a waiting camel. The entire operation took place at the double, with proper military discipline, as the Baron himself marched up and down smacking his whip against his boots as a reminder to anyone who didn't work fast enough that they would surely get a beating.

Soon the whole army was ready to go. About one thousand men galloped off across the flat grassland that sparkled with frost in the early morning sun. There was not a single cloud in the blue sky and the air was crystal clear, so they could see a vast distance in front of them. Far away on the skyline was a large range of grey mountains, and that was where they were heading.

The Bloody Baron rode on his white horse at the front of his army. He was feeling satisfied after hearing the future from the man in the black leather coat the previous night. This was the start of his Grand Plan. His army was going to capture Urga, the capital city of Mongolia, which had been under the rule of the Chinese for several years. Once he had defeated the Chinese army, he would rule Mongolia, a vast country sandwiched between Russia to the north and China to the south where most of the people were nomads, herding their animals through the steppes and deserts, carrying their felt tents with them wherever they went. Mongolians were very tough people. Every one of them learned to ride a horse before he could walk and was able to shoot a gun from the saddle with great accuracy. The Baron admired them for that.

Mongolia was to become the Baron's base. From here he would lead his men to conquer other countries, just like Ghengis Khan, a fearless Mongolian warrior king who, 700 years before, had conquered the largest empire the world had ever known – comprising Russia, most of China and large chunks of Europe. The Bloody Baron believed that he was the new Ghengis Khan and that nothing could stop him. He would be remembered as the greatest soldier of the 20th century.

He had been waiting for this moment ever since he had been a child growing up in a huge house in Estonia, a part of Russia on the shores of the Baltic Sea. There was madness in his family and he had been a terror from an early age. His father, who used to beat him regularly, ended his life in an insane asylum. Most of the boys in his class at school were frightened of the young Ungern and he never liked girls at all. Several of his classmates were forbidden by their mothers to talk to him. Consequently, he didn't have many friends. Once, when a boy showed Ungern his pet owl, the Baron tried to strangle it.

Even his schoolmasters found it difficult to control Ungern. He got into the habit of throwing his books out of the window in the middle of lessons, dashing out after them and never coming back. His masters didn't dare complain. The truth was that the Baron didn't like studying. He was already dreaming of being a soldier. One day, his sports master asked him: 'Look here, what do you want to be when you grow up?' The young Baron immediately replied, 'I'm going to be a great soldier, but if all else fails, I can become a sports master.' After that he was expelled.

His parents sent him to a military school instead, which he liked much better. But while he was training to be a cadet, a war broke out between Russia and Japan. Ungern asked to be sent to Siberia, where the fighting was. His request was turned down because he was only 18 and hadn't finished his training, but Ungern ran away and joined a division of Cossack cavalry, well known as the best horsemen in all of Russia. He was soon in the thick of the action. He was wounded several times but fought very bravely and was awarded an important medal: the Cross of Saint George. From that day forward he wore it round his neck at all times. He was wearing it this day as he galloped across the Mongolian plains leading his men towards Urga.

The Baron and his men had been heading towards Urga ever since leaving Siberia, a part of Russia, several weeks before. In 1921 Russia was in turmoil. There had been a revolution, followed by a civil war that had dragged on for more than three years. The revolution had been led by a group of Russians known as 'The Reds'. The Reds hated people like the Baron who lived in big houses and treated the Russian peasants badly. They had killed the Russian king, known as the Tsar, along with his entire family. They wanted a complete change in the way their country was ruled. Russia should be governed by ordinary people, they thought, not by men like the Baron, who was only important because he had been born into a noble family. The Reds had confiscated the Baron's house in Estonia, and many others like it all over Russia, and given them to ordinary peasants to live in.

The Reds had been fighting another group of Russians who called themselves 'The Whites'. The Baron and his men were Whites. They believed that

Russia should always be ruled by noblemen like the Baron. The Baron's White army had lost several battles to the Reds and had been forced to go to Mongolia.

When his men had captured Urga, however, the next part of the Baron's Grand Plan was to ride back into Russia and teach those Reds a lesson they would never forget. After several hours of hard riding, the Baron's army was nearing the great range of mountains. He held up his hand, the signal for his army to come to a halt, and pulled on his reins so that his horse would stop. A bitter winter wind whistled in the Baron's ears as he turned in his saddle and commanded his officers to join him.

When they were all gathered round him, the Baron had to shout to be heard above the wind. 'Beyond that mountain range lies a plain with a river,' he screamed, 'and beyond that lies Urga.'

All his officers nodded, and were secretly impressed that the Baron knew as much, because none of them had been in the Baron's tent the night before when the man in the black leather coat had read the bird bones. The officers were sent back to their divisions and the army began the long climb up the mountainside.

The going was tough, especially for the carts loaded with stoves, guns and ammunition, because the ground was steep and the frost had made it as hard as iron. And the higher they climbed, the windier it became.

However, the Baron was a fine horseman, and he galloped on ahead so that he would be the first to reach the mountain top. When he got there, the wind was blowing with the force of a gale, but the Baron didn't seem to notice. The first thing he saw was a small pile of rocks and stones. The tradition in Mongolia was for every traveller who crossed a mountain to add a stone to the pile as they passed. This was an offering to the gods who lived on the mountain and it was considered very bad luck for anyone passing not to add a stone to the mound. When the Baron's men caught him up he ordered every one of them to dismount and find a rock to put on the pile.

As the Baron's army filed past, each man leading his horse and throwing a stone on to the pile, the Baron took in the view in front of him. Down below he saw another vast plain, like the one they had just been riding over, with a river running through it.

Suddenly, there was the sound of a scuffle behind him and a shout. 'Your Excellency!' Teapot cried. 'This man refused to throw a stone.' As soon as the Baron heard the cry, the sabre scar on his forehead began to throb. Slowly, the Baron turned to fix the man in question with his eyes.

'Fifty lashes,' the Baron roared, and the man was dragged away to be beaten. The Baron returned his gaze to the plain after watching the first ten lashes. Beyond the plain was a line of hills and just on the other side of the hills the Baron could see hundreds of round white tents. Roughly in the middle of the tents sat a large building with a roof that sparkled golden in the sunlight. As the screams of the beaten man were carried past him on the icy wind, the Baron realised that here, at last, was the city of Urga and the sparkling roof of the Sacred Monastery.

Little by little, the Bloody Baron's long moustache began to twitch. Bit by bit, the Baron's face took on what was for him a most unusual expression. He had begun to smile.

Chapter Three

'Thinking is for weaklings'

The Baron ordered his men to stop and set up camp along the river in the plain because this was where the man in the black coat had told him he must wait before attacking Urga. Gangs of his men unloaded the stoves, guns and ammunition from the carts while members of the Baron's personal bodyguard set up their leader's tent under Teapot's supervision.

The sheep were left to find what grass they could between the sand and stones and patches of snow. A group of men was ordered to break the ice on the river so that they could get water for tea and another team marched off to collect firewood from the few small bushes that grew along the riverbank. There were no trees at all in the plain. When the men had gathered all the firewood they could find, they saddled their horses once more and rode out in search of animal dung which made excellent fuel because it burned slowly and gave off lots of heat.

For seven days and seven nights the Bloody Baron's army waited. Most of the men slept outside around the campfires, waking each morning at dawn because the fires had burned down and the cold made it impossible to sleep for longer. It felt like thousands of pins being stuck into their bodies.

In the mornings the men practised fighting with their bayonets, thrusting them into blocks of wood, and in the afternoons they had shooting competitions. The Baron's army was made up of men from all over the great continent of Asia. There was a division of Japanese soldiers and another of Russians. Tibetans made up a third division and the fourth consisted of Mongolian bandits whom the Baron had recruited during the long ride from Siberia. The Japanese were the most accurate shots while the Mongolians were the best horsemen. The Tibetans ate their dinner out of human skulls decorated with silver and gold around their rims, but the Russians were the fiercest fighters. This was because they had been fighting for so long that they were no longer afraid of dying. In fact, many of them thought it might actually be nicer to die in battle rather than continue living in Mongolia, where it was always so cold and uncom-fortable.

None of the Baron's men had undressed for many weeks because it was so cold. They hadn't washed either, because the Baron considered that only cowards washed and he had no room for cowards in his army. Consequently, all of them were very dirty. Most of the men also had rotten teeth. Their meals consisted mostly of dried meat, usually mutton, sometimes camel, and occasionally bear. The meat was very tough and almost impossible to eat with rotten teeth, so the men cut it up with their knives into small pieces and dropped them into bowls of tea, often with a bit of flour and salt added. Only on special occasions did the Baron allow a sheep to be slaughtered so that his men could eat fresh meat.

Many of the Baron's men didn't like the waiting. They also hated being cold all the time, they were bored of the food and some of them didn't like being filthy dirty. One night, a small group decided to run away. When the Bloody Baron discovered they were missing the next morning he flew into a furious temper. He threw his whip on the ground and began to jump on it.

Screaming and shouting, he sent the Mongolian bandits after them. Some hours later, the bandits returned leading the deserters tied up on their horses. The Bloody Baron had them all beaten with bamboo whips until they could not even stand up. Then he had them thrown into the river to drown. No one ran away again after that.

***

Early every morning, the Baron went for a swim in the river, diving straight in through the thin layer of ice that had frozen during the night and swimming into the middle with strong strokes. On the morning of the sixth day he stripped off as usual and marched down to the riverbank. He was preoccupied because he had been thinking about what the man in the black coat had meant about the hills around Urga being set alight with a thousand fires, and the Baron hated thinking. Even when he was at school he had hated thinking. Whenever a master asked him to think, he always said, 'Thinking is for weaklings. I'm a man of action.' But the Baron couldn't avoid the need to think about the thousand fires, and try as he might he couldn't work out what this part of the prophesy meant.

After his swim, he called a meeting of his officers in his tent. Colonel Sepailoff had just returned from a reconnaissance of Urga and had prepared a report.

He and a small band of men had climbed the hills surrounding the city. From there, they had surveyed Urga from the safety of the thick forests that covered the hilltops, before riding back through the night to the Baron's camp.

'We watched all day,' announced Colonel Sepailoff, who always spluttered as he spoke. He had a head that was rather too big for his thin neck and eyes like those of a dead fish. 'The Chinese defence force is stationed at the western end of the city. We counted the soldiers as they patrolled the streets below us.' A low gurgling sound rose up from Sepailoff's throat, which was his way of giggling.

'They were so close I could almost have reached out and grabbed them by their necks,' he continued, rubbing his hands together. 'They lack discipline. They're a shambles. I shall enjoy strangling them when the time comes.'

'How many are they?' barked the Baron.

'About six thousand, Your Excellency,' Sepailoff replied, still rubbing his hands.

The Baron started pacing up and down, smacking his whip against his boots as usual. Six thousand Chinese troops meant that the Baron's army was outnumbered by six to one. This called for a cunning plan. Suddenly, it came to him.

'Listen all of you,' he ordered, and the officers gathered closer to hear what the Bloody Baron had to say.

Chapter Four

The flames of a thousand fires

The Bloody Baron's plan was a clever one and it came in two parts. The first part, which involved the thousand fires that the man in the black coat had predicted, started that very night. The Baron sent all his men up into the forest on the hills overlooking Urga, from where Colonel Sepailoff had made his reconnaissance. Each man was ordered to build a large fire. When all the fires were ready, a signal was sent, and each man set his fire alight. Soon the hills around Urga were lit up by the flames of a thousand fires.

Down in the city itself, the Chinese soldiers gazed in awe at the blazing hillsides. They thought that each fire must be surrounded by at least ten men, probably having their dinner before attacking the following day. That meant, so the Chinese thought, that the Baron's army must be at least ten thousand-strong. They were wrong of course, but it didn't matter. The Chinese thought that they were outnumbered, and it's the thought that counts. They all started feeling afraid. The first part of the Bloody Baron's plan had been a success.

The Chinese commanders immediately called a meeting. They had to decide where the Baron's army would attack, and set up their defences accordingly. The Chinese had been in control of Urga for several years, and they knew the surrounding area very well. One of the first things they had done when they captured the city was to put the Mongolians' leader in prison at the top of the highest hill, a hill so high and steep that it was almost a mountain. It was virtually impossible to climb, so the Chinese commanders knew that the Baron's attack would never come from this direction. They agreed not to station many men at this end of the Chinese part of the city.

This was the Chinese soldiers' second big mistake because the next part of the Bloody Baron's plan was to launch his attack over that very hill. The Baron knew that the Chinese would consider such an attack impossible so it would give him the advantage of springing a surprise. And he knew from long experience that surprise was a very valuable thing to have in a battle.

There was also another reason for launching his attack over the highest hill. The Baron reckoned that if he could set free the imprisoned Mongolian leader, then the Mongolians in Urga would rise up and attack the Chinese themselves, so helping the Baron's army.

The Baron was right about the Mongolians helping him. They were rather pleased when they saw the fires on the hills surrounding their city because they knew it meant that the Baron's army would soon attack. The Mongolians had hated the Chinese ever since they had put the Mongolian leader in prison. Their leader was no ordinary man. For the Mongolians, who were Buddhists, he was like a high priest, and a king, and a god, all rolled into one. He was called His Holiness Bogd Jebtsun Damba Khutuktu, Khan of Outer Mongolia, or the Bogd Khan for short – the Living God of Urga. For the Chinese to take him from the Sacred Monastery and lock him up in a prison at the top of a hill was the very height of bad manners.

That night, while the fires burnt on the hillsides surrounding Urga, the Bloody Baron, Teapot, Colonel Sepailoff and a hand-picked band of the toughest Russian soldiers crept up through the dense forest on the hill where the Chinese were holding the Bogd Khan prisoner. It was an extremely difficult climb. The rocks were all covered in a thick layer of ice and were very slippery.

Towards the top of the hill the trees were so close together that the men could scarcely even see each other.

But the daring climb was worth it. They took the Chinese soldiers guarding the Bogd Khan by complete surprise and successfully stormed the prison. Some priests, who were known as 'lamas', helped the Bogd Khan on to a horse and led him away to safety as fierce hand-to-hand fighting continued all around them on the hillside.

Spurred on by their success, the Bloody Baron and his men soon overpowered the remaining Chinese and took all their machine-guns and ammunition. They then charged down the hill towards the city of Urga. The Baron's men hurtled past streets lined with tents inhabited by Mongolians, heading for the proper buildings in the Chinese part of the city. As they ran, they were joined by Mongolians carrying any weapon they could lay their hands on. Some carried sticks, others brought bows and arrows. As the soldiers and their new Mongolian allies approached the Chinese zone, the noise of the battle became deafening. Men were shouting and guns blasting. Hand grenades were exploding and machine-guns kept up a constant deadly chatter – the whole mad scene lit up by the thousand fires still burning on the hillsides all around the city.

Divisions of the Bloody Baron's cavalry were now attacking the Chinese garrison from the other side. They used hand grenades to blast open the gates, doors and windows. It was the end of the Chinese resistance. The Baron's army stormed inside and started to massacre every Chinese soldier they met.

As the sun began to rise, the Bloody Baron's conquering army got down to plundering the city. Fired by their victory after the long cold nights of waiting in the steppe, they went wild with excitement. They broke down the doors of shops and galloped inside on their horses to steal anything they could find. Inside a clothes shop, some men tore off the filthy rags they were wearing and wrapped themselves in rich silk coats. Another group found a shop that sold vodka and drank as much as they could. The drunken horsemen then rode up and down the streets shooting and killing anyone they came across. One Russian began shooting his own men by mistake, until he was shot himself. Colonel Sepailoff and Teapot found plenty of people to strangle.

Some of the Mongolian bandits, mean-while, had discovered the Chinese bank, a large two-storey building in the middle of the city's Chinese zone. A couple of hand grenades soon dealt with the heavy iron front doors and they rushed through them. Immediately inside, they stopped dead in their tracks.

In front of them stood a long sweeping staircase leading up to the first floor. The bandits, who had lived in felt tents all their lives, had never seen stairs before and didn't know what they were. The bravest among them advanced towards the first step. He prodded it with his sabre and when nothing happened he knelt down to sniff it. The step smelled of mutton fat, a familiar smell to all Mongolians. Carefully, the man put a foot on the bottom step. Still full of suspicion, he started to climb slowly upwards, followed by his fellow bandits.

When they got to the top of the staircase, they were amazed to find the first floor. Several of the bandits leaned over the banisters to look back down below. They were standing on a piece of ground that floated in the air, truly a wondrous invention.

Full of glee at their fantastic discovery, the bandits ransacked the bank's first floor office. They smashed all the windows before they found the safety deposit boxes and formed a line in front of them. Each man was allowed to plunge his bloody hand inside a box and keep whatever he found. Some were lucky enough to find gold coins. Others got silver, but most found only paper money which they immediately threw out of the windows as worthless. Then they grabbed armfuls of files from the desks, and flung them out through the windows. Outside in the street, thousands of notes, bills, receipts, and other bits of paper that banks tend to be full of, fluttered down to the ground in the early morning sun. The clouds of paper made it look like a holiday had been declared.

Chapter Five

The punishments begin

The plunder of Urga continued for three whole days. On the morning of the fourth day, the Bloody Baron called a halt. In the middle of the city, his bodyguards pitched his tent, which he made his head-quarters. From the tent he issued an order saying that anyone now caught stealing or harming the local population would be hanged; and any man found drunk would be punished by beating with bamboo poles: 100 lashes for officers, 50 for privates, and 25 for civilians.

The first thing that had to be done was to clear up all the dead bodies. They were loaded on to carts and taken to the cemetery on the edge of the city. This was no ordinary cemetery because no one was actually buried there. When a Mongolian died, the body was simply carried to this place and left there to be eaten by wild dogs. The Mongolians were Buddhists who believed that when someone died their spirit would come back to earth in another body, perhaps as a person, maybe as an animal. But either way there was no need to keep the old body because it had served its purpose. A priest from one of Urga's temples had the job of clearing corpses from the city – he was known as the Church Boneman. Following the Bloody Baron's victory, though, there were far too many dead bodies for him alone to manage. So a division of troops was ordered to help him. The wild dogs that roamed the cemetery ate very well for several days. Other divisions of the Baron's army were ordered to clean up the blood from the streets and wash them with disinfectant.

While the great clear-up was continuing, the Bloody Baron himself paid a visit to the Bogd Khan, who had returned in ceremony to one of his many palaces. As he rode his horse up the street towards the wooden fence that surrounded the palace the Baron noticed a long queue of Mongolians. Like the Baron, they wanted to pay homage to the Living God of Urga, but as ordinary people they were not permitted actually to see him.

At the head of the patient queue, a holy rope made from camel's wool and horsehair hung over the fence. This was a very long rope and one end of it, the end that no one could see, was held in the hand of the Bogd Khan, who was sitting in his palace. Outside, the pilgrims knelt one at a time to hold the other end of the rope after handing a silk offering to a lama priest on duty. The holy rope car-ried the pilgrims' prayers to the Bogd Khan and His blessings back to the pilgrims. After making this direct communication with the Living God each pilgrim was handed a thin band of red cloth to tie around his neck as a sign.

The Baron galloped past the queue to be met at the gate by two lamas who told the Baron to leave his revolver, whip and sabre at the gate before they led him inside. They walked across a wide stretch of brown grass to a large door, painted with writhing dragons and flanked by two huge stone statues of turtles.

Once inside the palace, the lamas led the Baron along a corridor. There were small cages on the floor along the whole length of the corridor and inside the cages little grey and white animals scurried. The Baron didn't have time to look closely, but he thought the animals were guinea pigs. As they continued along the corridor, they passed an open door that led into a room full of musical instru-ments and clocks of all shapes and sizes. A little further on, another doorway revealed a room piled high to the ceiling with bicycles and all sorts of toys. The Baron passed several more rooms, one full of telephones, another full of pianos.

'His Holiness likes collecting things,' one of the lamas said to the Baron when he saw him looking wide-eyed through the doors.

At the end of the long corridor was a staircase and the three men walked up it. The first thing the Baron saw as they neared the top was a stuffed gorilla. It stood baring its teeth on one side of a doorway. On the other side sat a stuffed tiger, its green eyes looking straight at the Baron with a rather fierce expression. The two lamas opened the door to reveal a room full of multi-coloured flags and big rolls of silk that decorated the walls. Five stuffed penguins stood in one corner of the room and a full-sized stuffed crocodile hung on a piece of string from the ceiling. At the far end, perched on a large throne, holding the holy rope in one hand, sat the Bogd Khan.

The Bogd Khan was a stout old man with a heavy round face. He was dressed in a yellow silken

Mongolian coat that had very long arms and a black binding wrapped around his big tummy. His eyes were wide and staring, for he was blind.

The Baron walked slowly towards the throne and stopped at what he thought was a respectable distance away. He saluted the Bogd Khan, even though the Living God could not see him.

Baron von Ungern-Sternberg turned and whispered to one of the lamas, 'Tell His Holiness that I am gratified to see him and that I put myself and my men at his disposal.'

The Bogd Khan leaned towards the lama who relayed the message and then answered in a low, monotonous voice.

'What does he say?' Asked the Baron. The lama looked at him and replied, 'He says he's pleased to see you.'

Chapter Six

Teapot learns to drive

As the Bloody Baron left the Bogd Khan's palace he was feeling very satisfied. In thanks for saving Urga from the hated Chinese, the Bogd Khan had given the Baron a golden bridle for his horse and a yellow silk coat like the one the Living God himself had been wearing. The Baron was delighted with his new coat and hence-forth wore it wherever he went.

In the months following his victory, the Bloody Baron set about reorganising the city. He set up military schools, built bridges, introduced new money with his portrait on, and established a telephone system. His men were all much happier now that they had beds to sleep in and better food to put in their bellies. Winter passed, and spring had sprung. Birds appeared in Urga as if from nowhere and the grass, which had been brown and dusty throughout the long winter, became green and lush. It still got quite cold at night, but during the daytime the city was bright and warm.

Teapot found a Chinese merchant who owned a motorcar and asked him to come to the Baron's tent because the Baron wanted to buy the car. But the merchant had heard that Teapot was always present when the Baron gave an interview and if, during the course of conversation, the Baron requested a teapot, his adjutant would slink up behind the guest, suddenly grab him by the neck and strangle him to death. The merchant was so afraid of this happening that he simply gave Teapot the car, and the Bloody Baron took to being driven round the streets of Urga wearing his new yellow silk coat and his Cross of Saint George. Teapot had never driven a motorcar before, and wasn't particularly good at it, but he enjoyed driving immensely. As he drove, Teapot would whistle loudly through his teeth so that everyone knew the Baron was coming. He never whistled a tune, because he had never learned any, but just a single, high-pitched note. Everyone soon learned to recognise the approaching vehicle by the whistling and kept well clear, so there were never any accidents.

The Baron introduced some new laws for his men. Drunkenness was no longer punished by flogging. Instead, if the Baron happened to meet one of his men who was too smashed, he simply sent him to spend a day or two on the roof of the nearest house. The Chinese part of the city, where the troops were stationed, thus presented a very strange sight. Officers and men could be seen standing, sitting or lying down on virtually every rooftop. Some paced back and forth, others looked around or engaged in whispered conversation with the man on the nearest other roof. At night they could be seen curled up next to a chimney to keep warm.

The Bloody Baron's men thought this punishment was strange, but they had got used to the Baron's unusual methods. The Mongolians who lived in Urga also thought the men's behaviour was very peculiar, but they had other things to worry about.

The Baron had ordered public toilets to be built throughout the city because he was fed up with the Mongolian custom of relieving themselves in the street. Everywhere he drove, the Baron saw groups of Mongolians crouched down on the edge of the pavements and in side streets satisfying their needs. They always did so in groups so that they could chat to each other, but the Baron considered pooing in public very uncivilised and rather unhygienic.

In fact, the streets of Urga were not as dirty and

smelly as you might think because the wild dogs from the cemetery would prowl into the city at night and hoover up the human excrement. The Mongolian residents found this to be a very satisfactory arrangement. They argued that it was far better to have the dogs clean up the streets every night than to store all the poo in the middle of the city in these things called toilets.

The wild dogs also had another advantage. They not only acted like street cleaners but also like policemen, because they would attack any person walking the streets at night unless they carried an oil lamp. Anyone up to no good, and thus not wanting to be seen, ran the risk of being attacked by the savage dogs. Since no one wanted to be attacked by the dogs, there was very little crime in Urga.

But the Bloody Baron thought this was all wrong. He had appointed Colonel Sepailoff to be in charge of security in Urga and thus there was no need for wild dogs to be roaming the streets. Of course the Mongolians didn't think much of Colonel Sepailoff.

As soon as he was appointed, Sepailoff set up a special strangling unit consisting of him and five other soldiers, one of whom was called Hermann Bogdanoff, a silent man who had three fingers of his right hand missing. Their job was to creep around Urga on tiptoe looking for spies.

The Bloody Baron had become very worried about spies. Now that he effectively ruled Mongolia he was nervous about losing his power. As a leader the Baron was feared by all in Urga, but even the best leaders have their worries. Taking Mongolia was just the first stage of his Grand Plan and while he was reorganising Urga, he had started to work out the next stage. He had to keep control of Mongolia because it was from here that he would lead his army back into Russia to fight the Reds. If any spy learned of this plan, they would tell the Reds who would then be ready for him. So it was very important that all spies were eliminated. This was Colonel Sepailoff's main job.

Once the strangling unit had seen someone

they thought looked like a spy, one of them would engage the victim in conversation. Meanwhile the appointed executioner would approach him from behind and slip a noose around his neck or simply thrust out his two hands with the fingers spread wide. Colonel Sepailoff liked strangling people himself, but he enjoyed watching people being strangled even more. Whenever he could, he would lure the victim to a half open door so that he couldn't see the executioner creeping up behind. He would talk and talk until suddenly, as quick as lightning, ten fingers would appear and the victim would fall backwards. When there were only seven fingers, Sepailoff knew it was Hermann Bogdanoff.

Colonel Sepailoff also made good use of Urga's prison. This was a terrible place, one of the most horrible prisons in the world. It consisted of a few rooms that were piled with wooden boxes that looked like small coffins. Each box was just over a metre long and about half a metre high. They were the prisoners' cells. Inside each box, the prisoner could neither sit up nor lie down at full length. Their food was pushed through a small hole in the side of the box.

Sometimes, when Colonel Sepailoff was feeling particularly cruel, he would open a box and give the prisoner some cushions to make him more comfortable. Then he would close the box, pull the prisoner's arm out through the food hole, and tell the prisoner some jokes as he tied a leather bag containing a wild onion around the prisoner's hand. The bag was left like this for many weeks. Eventually, the onion began to go bad. As it did so, the onion produced acids that literally rotted the prisoner's hand away.

As the months passed, Urga's residents grew tired of the Bloody Baron and his army. They were terrified of Colonel Sepailoff and his gang of stranglers because too often it was innocent people who were accused of being spies and eliminated or taken to prison. Even the Bogd Khan became frightened of the Bloody Baron and lost confidence in him. He instructed his lamas to hide all the treasures of the Buddhist temples, just in case the Baron felt like stealing them.

Chapter Seven

'Death to the Reds!'

The morning of 13 May 1921 brought another fine sunny day to the city of Urga. Inside his tent, the Bloody Baron was putting the finishing touches to a new order. He had been up all night working on it and the floor of his tent was littered with earlier drafts that had gone wrong. But he was now pleased with the result. On the first sheet of the finished version were written the following words:

ORDER
To Russian detachments in the

territory of Soviet Siberia
No 15 given at Urga,
May 21st, 1921

I, Lieutenant-General Baron von Ungern-Sternberg, commanding the Asiatic cavalry division, bring the following to the notice of all Russian units ready to fight the Reds in Russia.

The Order covered several sides of paper. In it was a lot of talk about the Bloody Baron's Grand Plan. It said that the Baron's army would leave Urga and ride to Moscow, just as the great Mongolian warrior king Ghengis Khan had done 700 years before. On the way, the Baron's army would kill all Reds in their path. No mercy should be shown to the Reds, the Order stated, because they all had to be wiped out.

There were three curious things about the Baron's

Order. The first curious thing was that it was written down at all. None of the Baron's many previous orders had ever been written on paper. He had simply shouted them at the nearest man who had passed on the word to the rest of the army. So why then, you might ask, was this Order number 15 rather than Order number 1? This was the second curious thing.

The answer to this question was to be found the previous night, when the Baron had received another man in a black leather coat tied with small bells, wearing a bushy cap of animal hide and carrying a horsehead stick. As before, the man had read the bird bones and told the Bloody Baron that number 15 was a lucky number for him. Hence the Baron decided that this Order should be numbered 15.

The man in the black leather coat had also told the Baron that 21 was another lucky number. This explains the third curious thing about the Order, which is that the date the Baron had written on it was May 21st, while the real date was May 13th.

After checking over Order number 15 one final time, to make sure that it contained no spelling mistakes, the Bloody Baron gave it to Teapot and told him to have it copied a thousand times and sent to all parts of Mongolia. When Teapot had left the tent the Baron looked at all the bits of paper strewn about the floor. He stroked the ends of his long moustache, which had begun to twitch, and started lashing at the bits of paper repeatedly with his whip, shrieking 'DEATH TO THE REDS!' as he did so.

A few days later the Bloody Baron's army rode out of Urga with the Baron on his white horse at its head. The Baron wore his yellow silk coat and all his men looked surprisingly smart in new navy blue uniforms. Each man also carried a new sabre, a new gun and a new whip. Only Colonel Sepailoff and his strangling unit were left behind in Urga. They had secretly been told to kill any Russians who still remained in the city, because the Baron believed that if they hadn't joined his army they must be spies. There was no room for error if his Grand Plan was to be a success.

The army rode north, towards the part of Russia called Siberia. At last they were embarking on the second stage of the Bloody Baron's Grand Plan. The Baron was feeling very determined as he galloped across the steppe. He knew that defeating the Reds would not be an easy task, but his army had to succeed, or he would never reach Moscow and never again see his great house in Estonia. Crushing the Reds was what his dream of being the greatest soldier since Ghengis Khan depended on. All the men in his army were also eager to fight again after their long rest in Urga. They were excited at the prospect of killing Reds and plundering new towns and cities, which would make them rich.

Half a day's ride from the city they crossed the river where they had camped for seven days and seven nights before attacking Urga. Gazing at the river sparkling in the sunshine and the green grass of the plain awash with wild flowers, they could hardly believe it was the same place that had been so bitterly cold and windy just four months before.

They rode for more than a week across the lush plains as storks flew high above them in the brilliant blue sky. As they galloped across the grasslands, they were watched by small furry animals called marmots, that look like squirrels but with short tails. Marmots live in holes in the ground, where they hibernate all winter, but now that the weather was warm, they sat up on their back legs and chattered to each other as the horsemen thundered past.

The Bloody Baron's army crossed into Siberia and began fighting Reds wherever they found them. They attacked military posts and villages. When they attacked the first village, the Baron reckoned that all the villagers would fight on his side, because he assumed every-one hated the Reds as much as he did. But to his dismay, most of the villagers simply ran away into the forest to hide because they were tired of fighting and had heard that the Baron was a cruel tyrant. When the Baron and his army captured the village he rounded up all its remaining inhabitants and locked them into a barn. Then he set the barn alight and everyone inside died a horrible death in the flames.

'That will teach the others not to run away next time,' the Baron said.

For the next three months, the Bloody Baron kept attacking villages. His army killed many Reds and recorded many victories, but also lost many of their own men. By this time, their new navy blue uniforms looked like rags, but the men kept thinking of all the cities they would plunder before they reached Moscow, which drove them forward into every battle. Sometimes a horse would die in the fighting and the Baron had to take a replacement horse from a village. Having written out Order number 15, he considered writing things down to be a good thing, so each time he took a horse, he handed the villager a piece of paper, which read:

IOU ONE HORSE
PAYABLE WHEN WE REACH MOSCOW
SIGNED:

&

Fighting almost every day for months was a very tiring business, and one night, while the Baron's army were all sleeping very deeply in a clearing in a forest, they were attacked by a Red battalion. The Baron had posted some of his men to stand guard, but they were so exhausted they also fell asleep. So the Red attack took them all completely by surprise.

Half asleep and barely dressed, the Baron's ragged army ran for their lives. The Bloody Baron himself forgot to grab his yellow silk coat as he ran. He and his men only just had time to jump on to their horses and ride off, but they left behind all of their food, all of their ammunition, and most of their guns. Many of them were also wounded as the Reds shot at them while they were running.

After so many victories against the Reds, this surprise attack was a serious setback. The Baron's army had not tasted defeat since before they had captured Urga, vanquished the Chinese and conquered Mongolia. Tired, frightened and half-dressed, the remnants of the Baron's army had no choice but to retreat across a river back into Mongolia. The sense of shock they all felt lasted f or days. They became so hungry that they were forced to shoot some of their horses to eat. The men who had not had time to grab their boots when they were attacked cut up the saddles and tied the pieces of leather to their feet.

A feeling of gloom came down over all the survivors and their camp became a dismal place. Now it seemed that their dreams of riches would never come true. The Bloody Baron tried to maintain discipline by whipping any man who complained, but his men had become so depressed that even the threat of the Baron's beatings didn't make much difference.

One night, after the Baron had gone to bed, his men were sitting around the campfire when a Mongolian horseman rode up and told them all a piece of news that made them even more miserable. So depressed were they, in fact, that they all decided to run away.

Chapter Eight

'Did we kill him?'

To add to the Bloody Baron's troubles, things had not been going according to plan back in Mongolia either. Red Army units had been operating all over the region, and while the Baron's army had been fighting in Siberia, the Reds had invaded Mongolia behind their backs and captured Urga. They were now in control of the Mongolian capital. This was the news the Mongolian horseman recounted to the Bloody Baron's tattered army as they sat around the campfire that night. The horseman told the soldiers that Colonel Sepailoff had escaped and had ridden to China where he had been arrested by the Chinese army and thrown into a terrible Chinese prison. No one felt very sorry for Colonel Sepailoff, because none of the men had liked him or his gang of stranglers very much, but the news meant that they could not return to Urga for supplies. It was this realisation that made the men decide to run away.

Even though the Baron's soldiers were set on leaving the Bloody Baron, they were still frightened that he might come after them. Until, that is, one of the men suggested that they murder the Baron before they left. Everyone thought this was their only way out, and immediately they very quietly set up the one machine-gun they had left and aimed it at the Baron's tent.

All the men stood in silence with their eyes fixed on the tent as shadows thrown by the campfire flickered on its white felt walls. The man at the machine-gun squeezed his finger on the trigger and began firing. A jet of flames leapt from the machine-gun barrel as it spat its deadly bullets towards the Baron's tent. The noise of the shooting was deafening and hundreds of tiny holes erupted in the tent's walls, sending small bits of felt flying off in all directions.

Almost instantly, it seemed, the door of the tent flew open and the Baron charged out, dashing towards his white horse. He jumped on to his horse and galloped into the darkness. No one could quite believe what he saw. The man firing the machine-gun had seen the Baron disappear but he kept shooting at his now empty tent nevertheless. Then he took his finger off the trigger and silence fell once more around the campfire, although the soldiers' ears were still ringing with the sound of the machine-gun.

For a full minute nobody spoke. Then one of the soldiers whispered, 'Did we kill him?' But he knew very well that the answer was no. They all stood stock still in amazement at how the Bloody Baron had somehow managed to avoid all the bullets and escape.

Just at that moment, Teapot ran on to the scene. He stopped on the other side of the campfire to the men and looked in astonishment at his master's tent full of bullet holes.

'What's going on here?' he demanded in a dangerous-sounding voice.

The men turned to face Teapot. Slowly they started to walk towards him drawing their revolvers and sabres.

'Some target practice perhaps?' said Teapot, not sounding so dangerous now that the men were moving towards him. The leading soldier lifted his sabre high above his head as he neared Teapot.

'What do you think you're doing?' cried Teapot, now not sounding dangerous at all. 'How dare you?' he screamed as the sabre came down on his square head and a volley of shots rang out from a dozen revolvers.

Chapter Nine

'Who are you, stranger?'

The Bloody Baron had been in the middle of a dream about torturing someone when his men had opened fire on his tent with the machine-gun. His long life of adventure had taught him how to move very quickly, and he had leapt up from his blanket into the hail of bullets and had just had time to grab his whip as he kicked open the door and rushed out. Luckily for him, he also had his revolver because he always wore his revolver in its holster while he slept. However, since he had lost his yellow silk coat in the Red's surprise attack, he had taken to sleeping with only his trousers on, so he was bare-chested when he jumped on to his horse. The only thing he wore other than his trousers was his Cross of Saint George which he never took off.

As he was galloping off into the darkness, he assumed that his camp had been surprised again by the Reds. But when he heard the machine-gun stop and he realised that no one was chasing him, he reined in his horse and turned to face the camp. Not far off he could see the campfire and the gang of men stood around it. It was only then that the full realisation of what had just happened hit the Baron with a terrible force. The understanding that his very own men had tried to kill him made the sabre scar on his forehead begin to throb dreadfully. And slowly it dawned on him that perhaps this was the end of his Grand Plan, that his dream of crushing the Reds and of seeing his house in Estonia again might never come true.

As he glared through the darkness, he saw

another figure arrive on the scene and he heard his faithful adjutant Teapot scream, 'How dare you?'

The Baron whipped his horse and charged back towards the camp as a volley of shots rang out into the night. In just a couple of minutes the Baron was back and the soldiers who had just eliminated Teapot turned to face him. For a moment nobody moved. The men around the campfire were paralysed with fear. After so many months of obeying the Bloody Baron and calling him 'Your Excellency', they stood rooted to the spot in terror. They had been able to shoot the Bloody Baron while he was in his tent, but now that he sat on his horse in front of them, they were afraid even to look at him.

One man, however, plucked up the courage to lift his revolver and he fired a shot at the Baron. It hit him in the leg and the Baron's horse reared up as the Baron himself shrieked. 'You traitor,' he cried, in a terrible high-pitched scream. Then he turned his horse again and rode off once more into the night.

***

The following morning, the ragged men broke up into small groups and they all rode off in different directions, marking the end of the Bloody Baron's army. Several days later, in the middle of a grassy steppe, one of the groups spied a heap lying in the distance. They rode towards the heap and dismounted to inspect what they had found.

It was the Baron. He was lying on the grass, having slid from his horse, which was nowhere to be seen. Blood from his leg wound had seeped into the soil, making a dark patch in the green grass. Beside him lay his whip. He was unconscious.

One of his former soldiers removed the Baron's revolver from its holster and the rest of the group gathered round. They decided not to try to kill him, even though it would have been very easy to do this time. Mainly, this was because they were now pretty sure that the Bloody Baron could not be killed. After all, hadn't they all seen him run through a hail of machine-gun bullets and escape unhurt?

Finally they decided simply to tie up the Baron with very strong ropes and leave him where they'd found him in the steppe.

Several days later still, a Red patrol sent from Urga to survey the countryside came across a man tied up in the steppe. He wore no shirt, just trousers and a medal round his neck. He was wriggling about and rubbing his face in the dirt trying to get rid of the ants that were crawling all over him.

The leader of the patrol took off his cap, which had a red star on its peak, and wiped the sweat from his forehead with the back of his hand. He leaned over the neck of his horse and called out to the tied-up figure, 'Who are you, stranger?'

The figure rolled over to look up at the Red patrolman.

'I am Lieutenant-General Baron von Ungern-Sternberg, you stupid fool,' he screamed.

The men in the Red patrol were very startled at this. They had heard of the Bloody Baron and were afraid of his brutal repu-tation. They huddled round on their horses to discuss what they should do. Then the Bloody Baron saw the star on the head patrolman's cap and started shrieking 'DEATH TO THE REDS! DEATH TO THE REDS!'

This disturbed the patrolmen even more. But after a lengthy discussion they decided to arrest the Baron because they thought they might all get promotion for capturing such a dangerous man. Although they were still rather frightened of the Baron, they saw that the ropes around him had been tied very tight, so they didn't think he could possibly escape. They loaded him on to a horse and took him to the nearest town.

***

The summer of 1921 was coming to an end as the Bloody Baron was taken under guard from the town in Mongolia to Russia where he was put on a train and transported to the Siberian town of Novonikolayevsk. He was dressed in prison clothes, but his captors allowed him to keep his Cross of Saint George around his neck. The train stopped at all the major sta-tions along the line and at every station the Baron was paraded on the platform as an enemy of the people.

At the first station, dozens of Red soldiers were lined up along the platform and the Baron went berserk as soon as he saw them. He started struggling for all he was worth and shouting 'DEATH TO THE REDS!' So his guards tied some extra ropes around him and stuffed a gag into his mouth. After that, peasants and other villagers all along the railway line came from far and wide just to see the terrifying White general they had heard so much about.

At Novonikolayevsk, on 15 September, the Baron was put on trial before a judge. The courtroom was packed with hundreds of people – peasants, workers and soldiers from Russia, Siberia and Mongolia. Thousands more stood outside in the street waiting for the outcome of the trial. The Bloody Baron stood in court with his hands tied together in front of him and was charged with several counts of banditry and murder. As the trial continued, he grew angrier and angrier as he realised that this really was the end of his Grand Plan. The judge was a Red, the lawyers were Reds, the soldiers were Reds, even the peasants watching appeared to be Reds. The Baron was found guilty on every charge, all of which carried the death penalty.

When the judge asked the Bloody Baron if he had any final words, the Baron stood to attention and declared that he didn't recognise the right of this

Red court to try him. 'Ungerns have given other people orders for a thousand years,' he told the judge. 'We have never taken orders from anyone,' he continued, his voice getting louder 'and I refuse to accept the authority of "the people".' Then he said that he wasn't sorry for anything he had done to any of his thousands of victims. He slammed his hands down on the table in front of him and started to shout. 'They all got what they deserved,' he screamed, the veins on his sabre scar throbbing rapidly, 'because just like you lot, they were all too Red!'

The judge had heard enough and ordered the Baron to be taken away. He was escorted out into a muddy yard behind the court house where a Red Army firing squad was waiting. The Baron was placed in front of a brick wall and he stood there glaring at the men as they lined up in front of him.

A cool autumn wind began to blow as the officer in charge ordered the firing squad to take aim. A few moments later, Baron von Ungern-Sternberg died in a hail of bullets, his Cross of Saint George still hanging around his neck.

KEY DATES

1886 Baron von Ungern-Sternberg is born in Graz, Austria.

1899 The Baron's father is committed to an insane asylum.

1904 Russia goes to war with Japan and the Baron runs away to join the army where he is awarded the Cross of St. George for bravery in battle.

1909-14 The Baron receives a sabre cut on his head in a duel. He also first visits Mongolia.

1914 World War I begins.

1917 (October) The Reds win the revolution in Russia, but the defeated whites begin a civil war.

1920 The Baron enters Mongolia with his troops.

1921 (February) The Baron captures Urga.

1921 (September) Baron von Ungern-Sternberg is shot dead by a firing squad.

Acknowledgements

I am very grateful to the following for
their comments on an early draft of this book:
Alexine Lafeber, Fred Sculthorp, Jack Eardley,
Joe Rankine and Joshua O'Keefe.

Author biography

Nick Middleton teaches geography at Oxford University, and is the author of more than a dozen books, mostly on travel and environmental themes. He is also the presenter of Channel 4's *Extremes* series.

Dear Reader,

No matter how old you are, good books always leave you wanting to know more. If you have any questions you would like to ask the author, **Nick Middleton,** about **The Bloody Baron** please write to us at: SHORT BOOKS, 15 Highbury Terrace, London N5 1UP.

If you enjoyed this title, then you would probably enjoy others in the series. Why not click on our website for more information and see what the teachers are being told? **www.theshortbookco.com**

All the books in the WHO WAS… series are available from TBS, Distribution Centre, Colchester Road, Frating Green, Colchester, Essex CO7 7DW (Tel: 01206 255800), at £4.99 + P&P.

OTHER TITLES IN THE WHO WAS...SERIES

WHO WAS... Admiral Nelson
The Sailor Who Dared All to Win
Sam Llewellyn
1-904095-65-8

No one ever imagined that a weak skinny boy like Horatio Nelson would be able to survive the hardships of life at sea. But he did. In fact he grew up to become a great naval hero, the man who saved Britain from invasion by the dreaded Napoleon.

Nelson was someone who always did things his own way. He lost an eye and an arm in battle, but never let that hold him back. He was brilliant on ships, clumsy on land, ferocious in battle, knew fear but overcame it, and never, never took no for an answer.

This is his story.

WHO WAS... David Livingstone
The Legendary Explorer
Amanda Mitchison
1-904095-84-4

Born a poor Glasgow cotton-mill worker, David grew up to become a great explorer and hero of his time.

This is his incredible story. The tough man of Victorian Britain would stop at nothing in his determination to be the first white man to explore Afirca, even if it meant dragging his wife and children along with him.

He trekked hundreds of miles through dangerous territory, braving terrible illness and pain, and was attacked by cannibals, rampaging lions and killer ants...

WHO WAS... Anne Boleyn
The Queen Who Lost her Head
Laura Beatty
1-904095-78-X

For Anne Boleyn, King Henry VIII threw away his wife, outraged his people, chucked his religion, and drove his best friend to death.

What does it take to drive a King this crazy? Was she a witch? An enchantress? Whatever she was, Anne turned Tudor England upside-down and shook it. And everyone was talking about her...

But Anne lived dangerously. And when she could not give the King the one thing he wanted – a son – his love went out like a light. The consequences for Anne were deadly...

WHO WAS... Ada Lovelace
Computer Wizard of Victorian England
Lucy Lethbridge
1-904095-76-3

Daughter of the famous poet Lord Byron, Ada Lovelace was a child prodigy. Brilliant at maths, she read numbers like most people read words.

In 1834 she came to the attention of Charles Babbage, a scientist and technowhizz who had just built an amazing new 'THINKING MACHINE'. Ada and Mr Babbage made a perfect partnership, which produced the most important invention of the modern world – THE COMPUTER!

WINNER OF THE BLUE PETER BOOK AWARD 2002!

WHO WAS... Queen Victoria
The Woman who Ruled the World
Kate Hubbard
1-904095-82-8

Victoria was just 18 when she was crowned Queen in 1837 – a tiny figure with a will of iron. Never was there so queenly a queen. She made Britain great, and the people loved her for it.

In 1861 tragedy struck, when her husband Albert died. The little Queen loved dogs and cream cakes and the troops who fought her wars, but most of all she loved Albert. Dumb with grief, she hid herself away. Suddenly it seemed the woman who had made the monarchy so strong would destroy it. Could anyone persuade Victoria to be Queen again?

WHO WAS... Florence Nightingale
The Lady and the Lamp
Charlotte Moore
1-904095-83-6

Even as a little girl, Florence Nightingale knew she was different. Unlike the rest of her family, she wasn't interested in fancy clothes or grand parties. She knew God wanted her to do something different, something important... but what?

In 1854, shocking everyone, she set off to help save the thousands of British soldiers injured in the disastrous Crimean war. Nothing could have prepared her for the horror of the army hospital, where soldiers writhed in agony as rats scuttled around them on the bloodstained floor.

But Florence set to work, and became the greatest nurse the world had ever seen...

WHO WAS... Alexander Selkirk
Survivor on a Desert Island
Amanda Mitchison
1-904095-79-8

On the beach stood a wild thing waving its arms and hollering. The thing had the shape of a man, but it was all covered in fur, like a Barbary ape. What was it? A new kind of animal? A monster?

It was Alexander Selkirk, Scottish mariner and adventurer, thrilled to be rescued by passing sailors after four years alone on a Pacific island. This is the story of how Selkirk came to be stranded on the island and how he survived, the story of...

THE REAL ROBINSON CRUSOE.

Emily Davison
The girl who gave her life for her cause
Claudia FitzHerbert
1-904095-66-6

Sam Johnson
The wonderful word doctor
Andrew Billen
1-904095-77-1

Annie Oakley
Sharpshooter of the Wild West
Lucy Lethbridge
1-904095-60-7

Charlotte Brontë
The girl who turned her life into a book
Kate Hubbard
1-904095-80-1

Ned Kelly
Gangster hero of the Australian outback
Charlie Boxer
1-904095-61-5

William Shakespeare
The mystery of the world's greatest playwright
Rupert Christiansen
1-904095-81-X

Madame Tussaud
Waxwork queen of the French Revolution
Tony Thorne
1-904095-85-2

Nelson Mandela
The prisoner who became a president
Adrian Hadland
1-904095-86-0